SCANIA

Pat Kennett

WORLD TRUCKS NO 2

TRANSPORTATION SERIES

AZTEX
CORPORATION
7002 E. PASEO SAN ANDRES
TUCSON, ARIZONA 85710

AZTEX
CORPORATION

Front endpaper The pride of 41 men who helped build
the rugged Vabis trucks can be imagined as they posed for
this photograph in 1908. It was widely used in brochures
and advertisements at the time.

© Patrick Stephens Limited 1978

First published in 1978

Design by Tim McPhee

Printed in Great Britain
Library of Congress Catalog Card Number 78-53444
ISBN 0-89404-007-3

CONTENTS

AUTHOR'S PREFACE

When a company is as old as Scania—or indeed its partner, Vabis—with records and recollections going back well into the last century, it becomes difficult to establish what was actual fact and what was legend, growing from spectacular feats of engineering and transportation in those far off days. The task is not made easier by the several major re-organisations that happened over the years, not to mention a disastrous fire which all-but destroyed the factory around the time of the First World War. Furthermore, with engineers as inventive and prolific as were Scania's through the decades, the sheer volume of material involved is staggering. Consequently, I was more than grateful for an offer of help from my good friend Sven Nylin, who looks after the truck information office at Scania. Without his energetic pursuit of fact, as distinct from legend, and his persistance in tracking down early employees of the company who could help to establish that fact, this book could not have been completed.

With that inestimable help I have sought to paint a picture of Scania with broad and bold strokes, rather than minutely detailed pen work, illustrating the main trends of their products, the reasons for building them, the type of men who were responsible for the work, and the effects that the vehicles themselves had on the people and industry of the country as the years went by. If any reader's particular interest is neglected I crave forgiveness. Scanias are currently operating in more countries of the world than there are pages in this book, and for every scheduled production type built there was at least one non-standard special machine, often more. Nevertheless, the task of piecing together this jigsaw puzzle of engineering, human and commercial activity, proved to be a fascinating experience.

FIRST STEPS

As long ago as 1827 there was a small wagon factory in Södertälje, a Swedish town situated on an inlet of the Baltic, with the vast lake Mällaren stretching away into the Swedish interior and to Stockholm itself. Right through the middle of the 19th century a steady flow of wagons emerged from the factory for Sweden's expanding rail network. However, by the time 1890 came production was faltering because of a variety of economic problems and the large iron-manufacturing company of Surahammars Bruk, which had origins going right back to the 1500s, bought that small Södertälje factory and extended and modernised it.

In 1891 it was reopened as Vagnfabriks Aktie Bolaget in Södertälje, or the Wagon Factory Ltd in Södertälje. The quality of their wagons with the expertise of Surahammar behind them was excellent and the business thrived. The name was something of a mouthful, even for the Swedes, so the initials were used for references to the company and its products, which appeared as V.A.B.I.S. That title style appears on many documents well into the 20th century, and was eventually tidied up to read simply Vabis.

Vabis management were very conscious of the fact that railways were not the be-all and end-all of transport; indeed with Swedish rail networks complete no further large scale business could be foreseen. Having heard of new fangled motor vehicles in various parts of Europe, a senior engineer, Gustaf Eriksson, was sent out on a study tour in 1896 to see what this new potential means of transport was all about. In particular, he was enthused by what he found in Germany, France, and to a lesser extent Britain, and he came back with recommendations that Vabis should go into the internal combustion engined vehicle business seriously. He was nervous about the use of petrol or gasoline as a fuel however. He thought it was an unnecessarily dangerous material and set about producing his first engine to run on kerosene. That engine worked admirably, except that it was somewhat smoky and smelly, and its emissions did not please the company directors, who even then apparently were aware of environmental problems. An improved version was built, and experiments with starting on petrol and running on kerosene were tried with varying degrees of success. However, Eriksson was still unhappy about having petrol around, and when he built his first car in 1897, its twin cylinder horizontal engine was kerosene fuelled, and was started by means of a fireclay ignition bulb and a blowlamp. If that sounds a laborious process, it should be remembered that it was still a great deal quicker and more convenient than getting a steam vehicle going from cold. The first Vabis car was quite large, easily capable of taking four people with space for goods as well. It was tiller steered, with iron tyres on wooden wheels, and is preserved to this day in the Stockholm technical museum.

Rapid development took place in design, both from the point of view of passenger convenience and that of technical quality. In particular the problem of using petrol safely was overcome to Eriksson's satisfaction, and by the time the first Vabis truck was built in 1903, an advanced stage of design had been reached. That first goods vehicle, designed to carry 1500 kilograms of payload, but in fact capable of considerably more than that, had what is now a conventional front mounted radiator for its twin-cylinder 15 hp vee engine, which almost certainly was inspired by Benz's similar type, a recognisable bonnet over the engine, semi-elliptic springs, and shaft drive to the rear axle. It still had wooden wheels with iron tyres, but it otherwise looked and worked like a thoroughly modern truck. At the first international motor vehicle show ever held in Stockholm, which took place in the spring of that year, the Vabis was a major attraction, but so was another Swedish truck, built by a firm from Malmö in the deep south of Sweden, under the name of Scania.

The word Scania is the latin version of a Swedish word, Skåne, which is the name given to the southern-most county in Sweden. Just why that name was chosen remains shrouded in the mists of the late 19th century. What is quite clear is that in the early 1890s the English bicycle manufacturers, Humber, having sold their products very well in both Sweden and Denmark, set up a small cycle factory in Malmö, in Skåne county and within sight of Denmark across the Öresund straights between the Baltic and the North Sea. That factory was originally known as Swedish Humber AB, but just before the turn of the century it was split off to become independent of Humber, and began making vacuum cleaners, paper machinery and gear wheels as well as bicycles under the name of Maskinfabrics AB Scania. Very early in 1900 new cycle designs appeared, the type 1 for gentlemen and the type 2 for ladies. They were very expensive and the price represented something like six months' wages for an average industrial worker at that time. Clearly the machines were not intended for the mass markets! Motor cycles were built too, not really special motorcycle designs, but strengthened pedal cycles with French petrol engines bolted to the frames, fed by English Zenith carburettors, and driving via a twisted leather thong belt from a flywheel pulley to a larger pulley bolted to the back wheel. The important aspect of those motorcycles is that they gave the firm some valuable working experience with the then-new internal combustion engine. Like their contemporaries at Vabis, the Scania directors decided that they should enter the automobile business, and towards the end of 1901 their first car was built.

The instigator of that first design was the works superintendent Anton Svänsson, who with a senior engineer called Thorssin built an experimental car in 1901, which became known as 'Thorssin's car'. An improved version followed—known as 'Svänsson's car'. Both were clever designs with a three speed gearbox alongside the two-cylinder engine, and pneumatic tyres all round. From those prototypes production cars were evolved, and early in 1903 the type B with two cylinders and the type C with four cylinders were offered to the public. At that stage engines were purchased from Kämper Motoren-fabrik in Berlin, which allowed Scania to concentrate on chassis development, resulting in some remarkably advanced vehicles for the time. Rack and pinion steering and a central chassis lubrication system were two of their features. Scania also introduced demountable bodywork in 1903 with an arrangement whereby goods or passengers could be carried according to demand. One such vehicle was used by a drugstore owner in Stockholm until 1925, and is still preserved.

Scania turned their attention to truck design late in 1902 and in order to gain publicity for their new machine they drove it 650 kilometres to the 1903 Stockholm Motor Show over dirt roads which were in appalling condition at that time and obstructed by innumerable gates. They completed the trip in 32 hours which raised great excitement. It also raised Royal approval for at the motor show Crown Prince Gustaf ordered a Scania car and sold his Daimler. So at that first international show in Stockholm both Vabis and Scania stood side by side, both with solid achievement behind them. The automobile age had arrived in Sweden.

Both Vabis and Scania met with considerable success right from the start. Despite all the technical problems facing them and even though they were in rival positions at that first show in 1903, they found there was room for both of them in a country which had sufficient basic prosperity to nurture its own new industry. Although both firms continued to make cars for some time—particularly Scania—it was the goods vehicles which formed the backbone of output in the following years. Sweden's geography was largely responsible for that, with a land area about three times as great as Britain, a tenth of the population, and big distances between farms, timber mills and townships. The coming of the motor truck promised dramatic improvement in communication all over Sweden, consequently development was rapid.

Purchase of engines from Germany soon ceased at Scania and by the end of 1903 they had produced their own petrol engine design. Vabis, too, extended their engine range to a four-cylinder type and experimented with various types of transmission and brake layouts. There was a friendly rivalry between the two companies which was not without its benefits, but in the field of passenger cars it soon became apparent that the main rival was not the other Swedish maker but the mass produced cars from Chevrolet, Oldsmobile and Ford, which were very much cheaper than anything built in Sweden. So those cars that were built tended to be the 'top-of-the-market' limousines and phaetons. But it was the commercial vehicles which established the two firms as important motor manufacturers, even though production never exceeded 20 trucks a year.

In 1906 Vabis produced a two tonne shaft-driven truck which was later developed into a remarkably versatile chain-drive three-tonner and used for every imaginable application. These models became collectively known as type 5 and their technology was to last for many a year. Scania built these trucks with all the wheels mounted on ball bearings—the first in the world to do so—and in 1909 one carried a three tonne load from Mälmo to Stockholm, covering the 650 kilometres in 33 hours to win a Gold Medal award from the Royal Swedish Automobile Club. Both Vabis and Scania aroused the interest of the Swedish Post Office, mainly with light chassis on which vans were built, and so the concept of the post wagon was born. In later years these post wagons and post buses were to play a major part not only in the development of the manufacturers, but also the life style of countless Swedes all over the country.

By the end of the decade it was clear to the managements of both Vabis and Scania that they needed more production facilities, less variety of models and designs, and a major improvement in efficiency if they were to survive against the might of the imported American motor vehicles. The clear solution was to combine the resources of the Swedish makers and so, in the spring of 1911, Scania and Vabis merged to become Scania-Vabis Aktiebolaget, a name which survived until 1969.

To begin with, truck production continued with developments of the type 5 Vabis, which after it had been fitted with chain-drive instead of the original shaft drive, had proved to be a remarkably reliable and durable 20 hp truck. Considerable numbers were built with the Scania-Vabis badge while the engineers sorted out their joint ideas for new designs, and the old Vabis did yeoman service as a truck, a tipper, brewer's dray, post wagon, bus, or almost any other use that demanded sturdy reliable transport. It was without doubt one of the success stories of the decade. But like all good things it finally came to an end in 1913 when new, more up to date designs entered the production phase.

The early cycle catalogues showed high prices — about six months average wage in 1900 — and even then a freewheel was Kr20 extra. An interesting detail is that although weights were quoted in kilograms, dimensions are in inches.

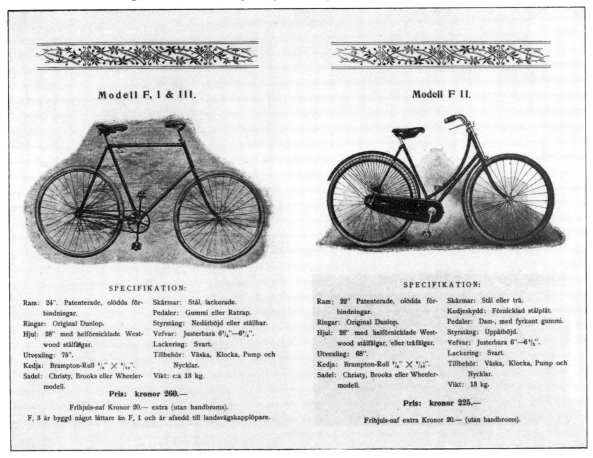

Modell F, I & III.

SPECIFIKATION:

Ram: 24". Patenterade, olödda förbindningar.
Ringar: Original Dunlop.
Hjul: 28" med helförnicklade Westwood stålfälgar.
Utvexling: 75".
Kedja: Brampton-Rull ⁵/₈" × ³/₁₆".
Sadel: Christy, Brooks eller Wheelermodell.

Skärmar: Stål, lackerade.
Pedaler: Gummi eller Ratrap.
Styrstång: Nedåtböjd eller ställbar.
Vefvar: Justerbara 6¹/₄"—6³/₄".
Lackering: Svart.
Tillbehör: Väska, Klocka, Pump och Nycklar.
Vikt: c:a 13 kg.

Pris: kronor 260.—

Frihjuls-naf Kronor 20.— extra (utan handbroms).
F, 3 är byggd något lättare än F, 1 och är afsedd till landsvägskapplöpare.

Modell F II.

SPECIFIKATION:

Ram: 22" Patenterade, olödda förbindningar.
Ringar: Original Dunlop.
Hjul: 28" med helförnicklade Westwood stålfälgar, eller träfälgar.
Utvexling: 68".
Kedja: Brampton-Rull ⁵/₈" × ³/₁₂".
Sadel: Christy, Brooks eller Wheelermodell.

Skärmar: Stål eller trä.
Kedjeskydd: Förnicklad stålplåt.
Pedaler: Dam-, med fyrkant gummi.
Styrstång: Uppåtböjd.
Vefvar: Justerbara 6"—6¹/₂".
Lackering: Svart.
Tillbehör: Väska, Klocka, Pump och Nycklar.
Vikt: 13 kg.

Pris: kronor 225.—

Frihjuls-naf extra Kronor 20.— (utan handbroms).

Early Scania motor vehicle ventures centred around motorised cycles. At that time—around 1901—they used bought-in engines, a policy which extended to the first cars and trucks.

Inset Origin of the famous Scania Vabis three spoke symbol lies in the sprocket wheel of the bicycles they made at the turn of the century. The symbol was used continually until the company became part of Saab Scania group in 1972.

Scania Motorvagn Typ B.

SPECIFIKATION:

Scania-Motorvagn för två personer samt plats för stort bagage eller också med löst säte baktill för en tredje person.

Motor inbyggd i främre delen af vagnen. stående encylindrig 4½ hkr. Normalt hvarfantal 1.000 i minuten.

Drifkraft: Benzin spec. vigt 0,680.

Tändning: accumulator, ställbar för tidig eller sen tändning.

Afkylning: medelst vattencirkulation genom rotationspump och rörkylare.

Förgasning: genom Longuemare originalförgasare.

2 hastigheter resp. 15 och 30 km. i timmen, 1 rörelse back. Igångsättning och hastighetsändring sker behagligt utan ryckning. För alla utvexlingarne finnes endast en häfstäng. Utvexlingen sker genom kugghjul och bakhjulen drifvas genom hvar sin kedja.

Fram- och bakhjul äro af trä och lika stora samt försedda med 1:ma gummiringar.

Vagnen är elegant lackerad och stoppad, färg efter önskan.

Pris: kronor 3,900,—

Scania-Motorvagn Typ C.

SPECIFIKATION:

Scania-Motorvagn för 4—5 personer utförd i tonneauform.

Motor: inbyggd i främre delen af vagnen, stående två- eller fyrcylindrig, normalt hvarfantal 860 pr minut, med regulator och reglerade insugnings-ventiler.

Drifkraft: Benzin spec. vikt 0,680.

Tändning: accumulator, ställbar för tidig eller sen tändning.

Afkylning: medelst vattencirkulation genom rotationspump och s. k. »Bienenkorb-kylapparat» med venti-lator.

Förgasning: genom Longuemare originalförgasare.

Två bromsinrättningar, som äro oberoende af hvarandra.

3 hastigheter framåt, resp. 42, 26 och 12 km. eller efter önskan, samt bakåtgång. Utvexlingen sker genom kugghjul, och bakhjulen drifvas genom hvar sin kedja. Igångsättning och hastighetsändring under åkningen sker behagligt utan ryckning. För alla ut-vexlingarne finnes endast en häfstäng. Fram- och bakhjulen äro af trä, lika stora och försedda med prima gummi-ringar. Elegant lackerad och stoppad, färg efter önskan.

Pris för 12—14 hkr. tvåcylindrig, kronor		9,000,—
» » 16—18 » fyrcylindrig, »		12,000,—
» » 20—24 » » »		15,000,—

Above Once the technology involved with the prototypes was mastered, Scania diversified, offering a cheap two-cylinder two-speed type B, and a bigger more expensive type C which could have two or four-cylinder engines to choice up to 24 hp. The upright front ends shown in these 1903 catalogue illustrations replaced the sloping cowl of the first type Bs.

Right The first car built by Vabis in 1897 was a big vehicle by con-temporary standards. The primitive design with iron tyres was soon superseded once the technicalities of the internal combustion engine were mastered. Gustaf Eriksson is at the controls with his managing director, P. Peterson, at his side.

These pages Scania's first car, like the Vabis, was quite a large vehicle and ran on pneumatic tyres. The chassis layout was very interesting with a two-cylinder engine on the left and huge gearbox alongside it. Drive was by a central chain to a different gear in a live axle. This machine was popularly known as 'Thorssin's car'.

Above There was no such thing as a production line in 1902 at Scania; cycles and cars were all assembled together. In the foreground is an early type B with an occasional four-seater body. Engines can be seen standing on the bench and at least five chassis are in course of construction.

Left By 1902 Vabis had sufficient technology to build a successful truck capable of carrying 1.5 tonnes with reliability. Although their cars by then used pneumatic tyres, the higher weight of the trucks dictated the use of iron, then solid rubber tyres for several years. Shaft-drive was used, not chains.

Above Illustrative of the practical approach of Scania's engineers is this type B car built with a goods-carrying compartment which could be replaced by seats at weekends. This particular machine was used by a Stockholm drugstore owner until 1925 and is now preserved.

Right Such was the confidence of its makers that the very first truck built by Scania was driven 650 kilometres over bad roads to appear at Sweden's first motor show in Stockholm in the spring of 1903.

Left There were many similarities between Scania and Vabis trucks in the 1900s, but Scania adopted the enclosed chain-drive while Vabis persevered with live axles. This is a Scania two tonner built around 1906 and a direct development of the 1.5 tonne 1902/1903 prototype.

Below Vabis' early truck design was simple and rugged and used a live axle, subsequently dropped in favour of the more reliable chains to each wheel. This example was built in 1907 and carried three tonnes.

Right From the earliest days advanced light commercials were built. This example, a Vabis half-ton meat van was made in 1911, complete with insulated and ventilated body.

Below The state of Swedish roads led Scania to fully enclose their engines and transmissions underneath the chassis. This commercial, built in 1909, carried dried milk from a plant in Nynas.

Left Scania built up an early export trade in northern Europe, and this tower wagon for the St Petersburg (now Leningrad) tram system was delivered in 1910.

Right Vabis truck chassis — the type 5 — were used for carrying passengers for many years. Often a chassis would have two bodies, one for freight, one for passengers, which could be changed over at weekends.

Below right Much of Scania's early commercial vehicle production involved vans and light trucks. This very elaborate newspaper van was built on a type G chassis in 1908.

Below One of the most successful Vabis trucks was the type 5 built from 1908 onwards. It formed the basis of most trucks built until well after the merger of Vabis and Scania.

Above Even in 1911 breweries liked to have specially built trucks, just as they still do today. This Scania, built for the Carlsberg brewery, had a very elaborate cab for its day and suspension which incorporated railway type coil springs in addition to the semi-elliptics. It also had electric lighting.

Left Heart of the type 5 Vabis was the 2.7 litre G42 engine which developed 20 bhp. It had an American Bosch magneto and an updraft carburettor of Vabis design. For 1908 it was a very advanced engine.

ENTERPRISE AND INVENTION

As soon as the merger took place both teams of engineers lost no time in pooling their resources to see what their combined potential could produce. The plant at Södertälje was adapted to build all the engines and most of the lighter vehicles including cars, while heavy trucks were concentrated at Malmö, where fire engine work was also done, and later, special bus designs developed. In those first few years after the merger the activity was nothing short of frenzied. In the nine years from 1911 to 1920 no less than 30 different engine types were designed and built. Not all of these were production units, of course, but it shows the resources and skill available.

Aircraft engines were included in the list, as were special marine types. One engine, a 50 horsepower V8 for luxury cars and express delivery vans based on similar chassis, was designed by the Danish subsidiary company in Copenhagen. But despite all that diverse activity, trucks remained the main commercial business. Late in 1912 a complete new range of trucks from 1.5 to 6 tonnes carrying capacity was launched, and these were in full production by the spring of 1913. They were characterised by a big domed brass radiator, handsome in the extreme, and a chain-drive to the back axle, enclosed in side cases to keep the mud out. The differential was in the gearbox which drove a transverse countershaft to which the chains were attached, and according to the capacity, engines ranged from 30 to 70 horsepower. By far the most successful and popular model in the range was the four-tonner with the 45 horsepower type 1545 engine.

The period marked successful ventures in export markets as well as at home, and as early as 1912 vehicles were exhibited as far away as Paris and Moscow. St Petersburg municipality featured among the important customers when Scania-Vabis supplied the tramway authority of that city with tower wagons to maintain the overhead gear,

beginning in 1910 and continuing for many years. There were branch companies in Norway, Holland and Denmark, while service support establishments were built in Russia, Australia and Siam, all before 1920. However, after the First World War trade in Europe was sorely depressed in contrast to the flourishing prewar years and in 1921 the Danish plant was closed and the production of engines and gearboxes there transferred to Södertälje. About the same time the Norwegian company, known as Norsk Automobilfabrik, was closed and replaced by a distributorship.

But the war produced something other than gloom and despondency. Although not directly involved in the hostilities, Sweden was obliged to secure her own defence and in 1916 a military four-wheel-drive truck, which also had four-wheel-steering, was designed and delivered to the Swedish army. The design was successful despite its strange appearance and not only did the army buy several for moving supplies in bad ground conditions, but a civilian version was developed that brought about spectacular improvements in mobility in the timber industries, especially in winter. So although the period up to the 1920s produced no great profitability, it left the company with a wealth of engineering and design know-how, soon to be exploited. Production had expanded spectacularly following the merger. Combined totals of Scania and Vabis trucks at the time of the merger was less than 40 a year, yet by the end of that decade an output of 275 trucks a year had been reached, or about one every working day.

The mechanical complexity of the machines developed rapidly too. The four-wheel-drive principle that had been developed for the army and extended to timber trucks was further developed in a lighter form for use in fire engines. As hard surfaced roads were still rare in Sweden a high mobility fire engine was a saleable proposition and 1919 saw the

first such machine built and sold. The transmission
layout was unusual in that an individual shaft went
to each wheel, to drive through a small worm unit,
each of the four shafts emerging from the main
gearbox through bevel drives. It worked remarkably
well and was not as heavy as some all-wheel-drive
types of that time.

Another major development was that of the
tandem drive bogie which first appeared in 1923. In
combination with large-section pneumatic tyres, this
made the transport of heavy loads in excess of twelve
tonnes a practical proposition for the first time.
Roads remained a major problem to all vehicle
operators however and local authorities struggled to
keep open roads which, when not frozen solid, were
deep in mud or dust. Scania-Vabis developed a
device which marked the start of major development
of a proper road system. They had already started
building hydraulic tipping gears some years before,
but in 1923 a design project was begun which aimed
to spread road making materials in even layers from
6mm to 36mm thick, working in conjunction with
the tipping gears on Scania-Vabis trucks. By 1925,
these machines, driven by the truck's rear wheels,
were in steady production and local authorities
bought them in quantity to build and maintain
proper roads. Sand, gravel, stone, and tarmaca-
dam could be handled, and that invention did more
to give Sweden proper roads than any other single
factor.

A double reduction axle was also developed, aimed
mainly at heavy truck use. It was so successful that it
killed off the chain-drive once and for all and,
among other things, allowed road speeds to increase
significantly from around 20-24 kph to well over
30 kph. Engine development was not neglected
either, and although nowhere near as many diverse
types were made as had been some years earlier, aero
engine production continued, and an overhead valve
engine appeared for the first time in 1920,
developing 36 horsepower. That was the type 1442,
and although it was not entirely satisfactory, its
successor, the 50 horsepower 1444 was extremely
popular.

All this time cars continued to be built, some of
them very elegant and elaborate. However, pressures
from the American makers forced the final cessation
of car production in 1924, and at the same time the
Malmö factory was closed and the Södertälje plant
expanded to make everything under one roof. That
point in history marks a major milestone in the story
both of Scania-Vabis and the vehicle industry in
general. What followed gave Sweden a design lead
over the world.

There was very little difference between the last pure Vabis
models (**above**—delivering milk in Stockholm) and the
first Scania Vabis types (**below**—with a farm body),
beyond the new joint name on the radiator. The old type 3
design remained in evidence.

Above right and right The first real Scania-Vabis designs
came in 1913 with a new chassis range boasting bold brass
radiators. Body and tyre equipment varied to customer
choice though the basic chassis were similar throughout.
There were versions of this design at various weights from
1.5 to 6 tonnes capacity, catalogued C, D, E, F, and G
types.

Opposite and above Even though five and six tonne payload trucks were built in 1916-19 the design retained some features from earlier years with chain-drive, solid tyres and in most cases open cabs.

Right Chassis plate on a 1913 C1c truck shows 30 hp output, two tonne payload and front and rear wheel capacities, which add up exactly to the gross weight. Clearly loading tolerance was an unknown science in 1913.

Below right For ten years after Scania and Vabis joined forces, the five litre 45-50 hp type 1545 was the most popular engine for trucks, buses, fire engines and even the larger passenger cars.

Overleaf

Background photograph Although volume heavy vehicle production became a reality in the last years up to 1920, the van business still flourished. The three Scania-Vabis 2121 vans on the left joined two earlier Vabis types in 1918 in a fleet run by a chain store group.

Left inset Bodywork seldom stayed as immaculate as this for long when the majority of roads were dirt surfaced. This 1916 chocolate delivery van was built on a type 2 Scania-Vabis car chassis.

Right inset Really heavy duty four-wheel-drive commercial trucks were built from 1917 onwards with a protruding front end to put as much weight as possible on the front wheels. As well as its own load, this one is hauling four trailers in winter conditions with chains on its wheels. There seem to be a lot of passengers too!

Left From 1912 on car radiators were delicately curved with a domed top tank. This style was retained until car building ended in 1924. Some larger cars had a vee-shaped radiator of similar profile.

Above Though of similar shape to the car radiator, trucks had a much wider and larger unit, with a square section top tank. This distinctive style was used up to the mid-1920s.

Left A simpler and less expensive truck radiator was evolved after the closure of the Malmo plant in 1924 and this style was retained throughout the 1940s with little change.

Above right The Danish subsidiary company grew quite large and even designed and built its own engines, including a 150 hp V8 type which was supplied to the main Swedish factories. Eight years after this 1916 engraving was done, the works closed down.

Right Balloon tyres, all-shaft drive and double reduction axles appeared in 1922-23 and were incorporated in models like this impressive 12 tonner. The ghost of the type 5 was finally dead.

Overleaf

Left As early as 1914 the combined Scania and Vabis activity extended to a very wide variety of transport. This is a dealer advertisement, published in Stockholm in 1914, extolling the virtues of all-Swedish manufacture.

Right Poster promoting Scania-Vabis exhibits at an exhibition in Göteborg emphasises the versatility of the vehicle range. The year was 1919.

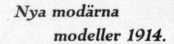

LEVERANS

till **låga priser** och **på goda villkor**

Svensk kvalitetstillverkning av
PERSON-, OMNIBUS-, AMBULANS-
och
LASTAUTOMOBILER

AKTIEBOLAGET
SCANIA-VABIS
SÖDERTÄLJE

*Besök vår utställning av olika automobiltyper i SVENSKA HALLEN
å Göteborgsutställningen – Utställningstelefon: Göteborg 114*

SCANIA-VABIS
СКАНІЯ-ВАБИСЪ

211

40 Hkr. Lyx-torpedlandaulet, levererad till H. K. H. Hertigen af Västergötland.
40 H. P. Torpedo Landaulet de Luxe delivered to   Роскошная ландолетъ въ 40 л. с. поставленная
H. R. H. Prince Carl of Sweden.   Е. К. В. Принцу Карлу Шведскому.

212

Samma vagn med suffletten nedfälld.
The same car with the hood dropped.   Тотъ же экипажъ со спущеннымъ суфлетомъ.

Left Evidence of the business done in Russia comes from this 1914 catalogue, issued by the regional dealer. The captions to the cars were printed in three languages.

Right After the merger the Malmo truck factory was reorganised and a long double assembly track installed. Production had grown to 275 trucks a year by the time this picture was taken in 1919.

Below The three spoke emblem which originated in the cycle sprocket wheel was applied to anything and everything appropriate; even the breather holes in some engine valve covers. The dealer sign became familiar all over Scandinavia.

Left Diversification made possible by the combined strength of the two companies led to the production of aero engines, the first of which was the 110 hp type 1661 built in 1916. Earlier attempts with a V4 aero engine were not successful.

Below Enclosed cabs became customary from around 1925 onwards. The type 1441 four-cylinder 70 hp overhead valve engine gave these trucks a higher peformance and the patented progressive spring was used to obtain good riding characteristics.

Right Overhead valves appeared as early as 1920 in the 36 hp 3.56 litre type 1442 engine. However, it only lasted five years and was never as popular as the 1545 side valve engine or its successor, the 50 hp 1445 model.

Below High power from four cylinders was a feature of the type 1441 70 hp engine fitted to both trucks and buses from 1927 onwards. There were six-cylinder versions too, one of which led to the development of the 'bulldog' bus.

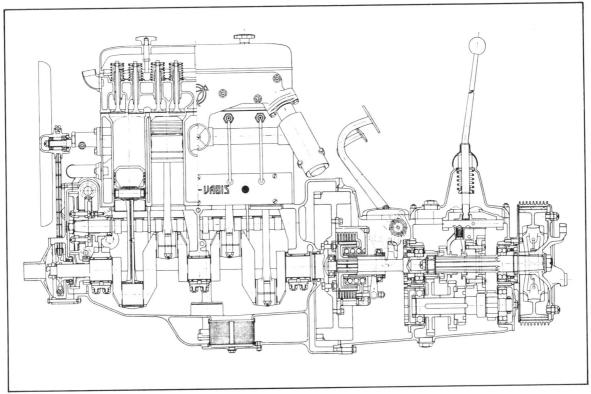

THE GREAT BUS YEARS

Since the early years buses had been built on the 5 type chassis and its later derivatives, but the concept of a truck chassis to carry passengers did not appeal to the management, particularly as the cars conveyed passengers in such luxury. So along with all the truck engineering development, engineers August Nilsson, Oskar Skogsberg and Algot Wiren were keeping their eyes open for ways to develop bus technology that would lift Scania from the world-wide ranks of vehicle makers who carried passengers on truck chassis.

The first step came in 1923 when research work that had been going on for some years into suspension design produced the Scania-Vabis patent progressive spring. Instead of normal shackles and pins the ends of this new spring were mounted under hardened cam blocks around which the ends of the top leaf rolled as load was added. When under light load, the mere tips of the spring touched the outer ends of the blocks. But as the load increased the spring deflected and the contact points moved inwards, shortening the effective spring length and moving the support points closer to the stiff section of the spring where numerous plates were clamped together. So automatically these springs gave a soft and gentle ride under light load, stiffening up under full load to give good stability and maintaining a smooth ride.

Another breakthrough was the double reduction axle already mentioned which enabled the bus chassis to be built lower, the small casing allowing a low floor level. So from the mid-1920s bus chassis at Scania began to take on a different appearance from their truck brethren. The result was dramatic. City and long-distance bus operators alike flocked to the Scania-Vabis works to see the new bus chassis. Despite the efforts of the road making trucks a long bus trip was still quite an uncomfortable experience and everyone was seeking an improved standard of comfort. The first model to use the new springs was a small one, seating 23 passengers only, but within a year 40-passenger types were being built, and not many years passed before long wheelbase machines seating over 60 passengers were offered for long-distance work. Bus production in the years of the late 1920s and early 1930s was as large as truck production. But there were still some surprises to come.

With Scania-Vabis firmly established as a specialist bus producer, the engine designers were looking for ways to contribute, in particular with quiet and smooth power units. The overhead valve 1400 series engines, originally built in four-cylinder forms, were extended to six-cylinders to give high power and smooth torque at relatively low engine speed. It was noticed that these engines were remarkably clean and compact, as well as smooth and powerful, so a special bus version was built with its auxiliaries located so that they took up as little space as possible. The result was a very narrow engine that suited the bus engineers ideally. For years they had been looking at the wasted space around the front of their bonneted bus chassis, wondering how to use it while the area further back was crammed to capacity with passengers.

The first step was the 'semi-bulldog' type, and just before Christmas in 1929 a bus with the engine alongside the driver instead of in front of him, was completed. But that was only an interim stage. Where manufacturers elsewhere in Europe, notably in Britain, were content to build the half-cab type bus for many years, Scania-Vabis wanted more. Despite the maximum legal width being 2.05 metres (6 feet 9 in) they reckoned that their type 1461 engine allowed space for useful bodywork on both sides. Careful shaping of wheel arches was necessary, but in 1931 the first full-fronted 'bulldog' type bus was complete, with the driver on one side of the engine and passenger seats over the wheel arch opposite. Immediately several large orders were placed and by early 1932 the 'bulldog' was in full production. Some operators used the forward space for luggage, particularly on long journey work, while others located passenger seats there.

Those front seats were the delight of children who competed for the privilege of sitting up front near the driver and with the finest view of the road ahead. A further advantage was that weight distribution was almost ideal and the progressive suspension could really work well. After that very few bonneted buses were built at Scania-Vabis and the 'bulldog' won a sizable export trade. It was not until many years later that a true full-front bus with usable space up front was developed by any other manufacturer.

From the very early days of van and truck production the Swedish post office took a great interest in the new motor vehicles. Up to that time they had relied on the limited rail network and inland shipping to reach the remote interior areas, with local journeys from the rail and pier heads undertaken by horses. All that meant that the collection and delivery of mail was a slow process and limited in its capacity. In the motor vehicle they saw a potential that perhaps even the manufacturers did not entirely envisage at that time. Not only could a motor vehicle carry mail much quicker than the ships and horses, they argued, but in many instances it could carry more too.

To begin with they purchased vans and trucks for mail deliveries centred round the big cities with their growing suburbs, but by 1913-14 they were looking at a wider concept. They calculated that if mail had to be carried between towns and villages out in the provinces and rural areas, they could carry other things too, like people and their baggage, business documents and packages that might not be entrusted to the mail. The concept was clear enough. But in those days of bad roads, and of course the weather in winter time was always bad, how could a regular reliable service be maintained? Experiments with various wheels and tyres were tried, and it was found that the mud problem could be beaten with up-to-date equipment. But deep snow was a different matter. There just wasn't enough power to use a snowplough on the front of the post bus. Then their chief engineer hit upon an idea. If they couldn't cut through the snow, why not go over it?

They went to Södertälje with their ideas and talked to engineers like Tage Söderberg and John Lionell. Could it be done? The answer was yes, and within a few months one of the strangest vehicles ever to emerge from the factory was wheeled out, its yellow paint gleaming in autumn sunshine. It was the first all-weather post bus, based on a 36 horsepower chassis. At the back it had cut-away wheel arches and special brackets either side of the wheels to carry 'Caterpillar-type' tracks. These were about 35 cm wide and carried on two bogie wheels each side. At the front, skis were bolted to the wheels and they steered with the front wheels. Both tracks and skis could be quickly detached. The body was a spacious affair with seats down the sides and lots of room for bulky parcels. It looked strange, but was an instant success, and for the first time the Swedish interior had a reliable winter communications service.

The post bus grew rapidly in stature and utilisation. What had begun as a regional service near the larger towns spread to the entire country by 1924. Soon special post buses were being built to suit particular areas, many capable of pushing a snow plough ahead, and these were mainly used in the southern regions. Skis still featured in the north however. The powerful 90 and 110 horsepower engines were frequently used and, of course, the 'bulldog' chassis when it appeared in 1932 was seized upon as an opportunity to get more capacity into a smaller vehicle. Size was always a critical factor in rural areas. As the concept developed, banking facilities and other services like mobile radio-telephone systems were added, particularly in the remote areas. The post bus therefore made a major change in the way of life in a large proportion of rural Sweden and remains an integral part of the life style.

Overleaf

Background photograph First step towards using all the chassis space was the type 8501 half-cab bus of 1929. It bore a remarkable resemblance to the Leyland Lion bus, but in fact Scania-Vabis went a step ahead of all their competitors with the 'bulldog' bus in 1931.

Left inset The engine of the advanced 'bulldog' bus was the 90 hp type 1461 six-cylinder unit. It was an unusually narrow engine, with bore and stroke of 95 x 136 mm and this compact size made the full-forward-style body a practical proposition, with usable room on both sides of the engine cover.

Right inset Up to the late 1920s all bus chassis had forward engine locations like this type B1-8405 bus working in Stockholm.

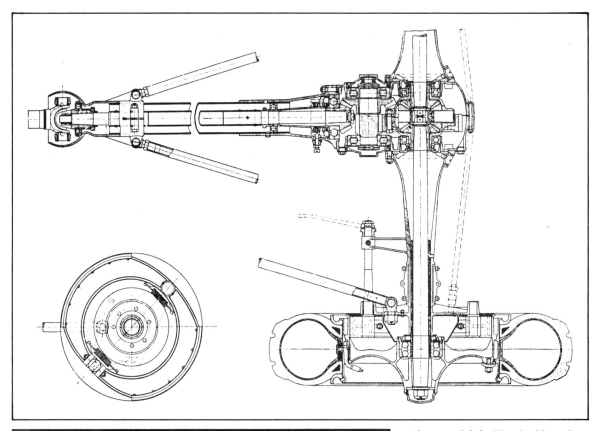

Above and left The double reduction axle opened up all kinds of possibilities from lower floors in buses to higher speeds in trucks. It was both compact and durable, even under severe overload.

Above right Revolutionary layout of the 'bulldog' bus with the driver on one side of the engine and passenger seats opposite gave a higher passenger capacity than any other bus within a given length. These buses were built in quantity for bus companies all over Scandinavia. This is the first one, the type 8305, built in 1932 with single tyres front and rear.

Right Private operators gave good value to their passengers. There is a certain similarity of style between this 1936 Scania-Vabis 8416 coach and the Leylands run by Southdown Motor Services in Britain at the same period.

Background photograph
Bus travel was fast and comfortable in the 1930s. These
five Scania-Vabis express buses worked on contract with
Swedish railways, who still operate an extensive road
network.

Inset
The production 'bulldog' chassis from 1932 onwards were extremely modern designs, pre-dating their competitors by 10 years or more. The drawing shows the 5 metre wheelbase, 37-seat chassis, while the photograph shows the 4.5 metre, 32-seat version. All had the 90 horsepower 1461 engine with the 110 hp 1546 engine coming in later versions from 1933.

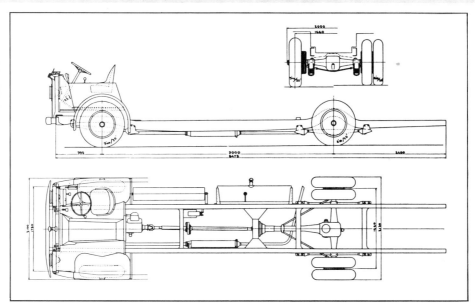

Left Early post wagons gave a boost to both sales and technology at Vabis. This very early fleet picture was taken in 1910 with a 2½ tonne 1907 machine on the right and two later, smaller types on pneumatic tyres. The post office led the trend toward proper cabs for the drivers.

Below By 1913 the Swedish Post Office was really developing its post wagon concept. These five Vabis van and six trucks were delivered in one batch in 1913 to Stockholm office. Note that even after the merger they still called Vabis vehicles.

Postautomobiler, Stockholm I, 1913.

THE GREAT BUS YEARS

Right By the early 1920s, the Post Office had the post bus service well developed, providing an elaborate communications system for large areas of the country. All weather operation was a priority, even in 1922, when the addition of skis and tracks enabled vehicles to travel in the worst snows. This was the first type specially developed as a post bus.

Below A superb 1913 Vabis (ie, built in the old V.A.B.I.S. works) post van is preserved in the Scania museum on the very site where it was originally built.

Left The years 1928-33 saw large numbers of powerful 90 hp post buses in use all over Sweden. Note that chains are fitted to one front wheel, a technique still used in winter by Swedish truck and bus men.

Right By 1940 post buses were working as mobile banks as well as all the other functions they performed. Mail bags were carried in a trailer in areas where there were large quantities of mail.

Below right The Swedish Post Office frequently led the way with technical innovation. In 1928 the type 8107 post bus had thermostatically controlled radiator shutters and 6-inch pneumatic tyres. The snowplough brackets are visible below the front bumper. Note the letterbox in the door.

Below The extra capacity and compact size of the 'bulldog' was welcomed by the Post Office and its good weight distribution gave superior handling on ice and snow. Interesting details are the manual assistance for the wipers and the rack on the front for cycles and other bulky items.

DIESEL TRUCKS AND SPECIALIST VEHICLES

Because of the enormous success of the various engineering developments in connection with the bus development programme, the truck activity for the first time since the early days of the company found itself in a secondary position. During the 1930s bus production exceeded truck output in several trading years, but that did not mean that truck engineering was neglected. The truck chassis were in any case modern designs with items like the progressive suspension, originally made for bus chassis, incorporated to bring a high degree of refinement. But whereas in Europe, particularly in Britain and Germany, there was a major transition to the oil engine, Scania-Vabis had remained loyal to the petrol engine. Demands from long distance truck and bus operators called for the cheaper oil fuel, but the company continued to concentrate on the petrol engine for many years.

In 1927 experiments were made with Scania-Vabis engines adapted to run on heavy oil. In common with a number of other manufacturers, including the new Volvo company founded that year, the man responsible for this development was Jonas Hesselman who had patented a means of running an engine on heavy fuel oil once it had been started and warmed up on petrol. By 1930 the first Hesselman-Scania engine was offered as a production option. It was called the type 1547 and developed a modest 65 horsepower. However, on long journeys into the interior of Sweden, its running cost was low and consequently it found a ready market, despite being rather more rough and noisy in operation than the current petrol engines.

Following the limited success of the Hesselman engine Scania-Vabis turned to the possibility of producing a true diesel engine which would start and run on heavy oil and produce economical power adequate for the heaviest trucks. Operators were beginning to get anxious about fuel costs with petrol, particularly those covering high mileages. It took quite a long time to develop an engine to adequate

standards and it was not until 1936 that the first Scania-Vabis production diesel appeared — almost ten years later than Gardner in Britain and MAN in Germany. It was an indirect injection design and was a very good engine when it finally appeared, very quiet and smooth, and developing 120 horsepower from 7.75 litres at 2000 rpm. Its success was immediate, and petrol engine production was cut by 75 per cent in a couple of years, so great was the demand for the new diesel. Buses, trucks, fire engines, everything, were powered by the new type 16641 engine which had pre-combustion chambers and heater plugs to aid starting. Rubber engine mountings were incorporated with the new diesel which added to its smoothness. The big petrol engines were subsequently confined largely to military vehicles.

That engine remained the standard heavy vehicle power unit for over ten years, although development of a new range of direct injection diesels began in 1939. These were known as 'unit engines' because the design catered for four, six, or eight-cylinder versions all to the same basic dimensions, with interchangable pistons, valves and connecting rods. Oddly enough, the biggest engines appeared first, with an eight inline type as early as 1939, followed by a six-cylinder version in 1942, and a four-cylinder in 1944. However, these were very limited in quantity and it was not until 1949 that volume production of these engines began as the D-series of power units. These direct injection diesels were highly successful and had a habit of running over 400,000 kilometres without major attention. In fact a 'Golden Globe' award was offered at one time for trucks that had covered that distance or more, the equivalent of ten times round the world. However the award scheme was quietly discontinued when it was discovered that certain claimants' figures did not entirely correspond with the declarations made to the authorities on their kilometre-tax returns! The D-series engine was one of the first in the world to appear in production as a turbocharged unit. Brown Boveri did the blower work and the eight-cylinder D815 was made to develop 205 horsepower. Scania-Vabis had entered the turbo-diesel era. That was in 1951.

In those immediate postwar years there was a technical and commercial liaison with Leyland, the major British manufacturer at that time. Some Leyland engines were imported but very few were in fact sold and most of them went back to Britain. However, a great deal of technical interchange went on, Leyland introducing technology on injection, cooling and the like, while the Swedish partners chipped in a lot of metallurgical casting know-how. Liaisons of that sort were not confined to engines however. Although the 'bulldog' bus had put Scania-Vabis ahead of the competition in the 1930s the rest of the world had caught up, or even overtaken them by the late 1940s, and new ideas were needed in the bus field as a matter of urgency. Accordingly an agreement was made with Mack in Allentown, USA whereby cooperation on bus technology would be exchanged for engine and gearbox know-how.

The first major fruit of that arrangement took the shape of a Mack city bus which was shipped to Sweden in 1951. This formed the basis of operational and production research for the next two years. As a direct result the Scania-Vabis C50 'Metropol' bus appeared as a production machine in 1953 and was an immediate success with Swedish bus users. From that design a whole series of modern buses has been developed suitable for world wide markets. Mack's gearboxes, even in the mid-1970s still bear signs of their Scania origins, especially the auxiliary types with their two shift levers, which was a Scania feature in the 1950s. Mack still use Scania engines in special applications, especially those where very stringent pollution regulations apply.

Back in the engine development arena things were not standing still. Successful though the D-series were, bigger and more powerful units would soon be needed and in 1958 the first of a new generation of engines appeared, the D10. It was a 10.25 litre unit developing 165 bhp and the following year a smaller D7 version appeared, designed on similar lines. These two engines were developed into the D11 and D8 types a couple of years later and turbocharged versions known as the DS11 and DS8 were added. Versions and developments of that same basic design still serve Scania well today. For example, the original D11 of 190 horsepower was the direct antecedant of the DS11.02 which develops 305 bhp with remarkable fuel economy. Similar developments affected the little D8 which in its most powerful form now develops 210 horsepower against the 120 horsepower of the original. In 1969 another new big diesel was introduced, the V8 14

litre DS14 type. That started life with just over 300 horsepower and has been developed over the years to produce 375 horsepower in 1977.

Data on D10 and DS10 engines, 1958

Type	D10	DS10
Cylinders	6 inline	6 inline
Power, hp/rpm	165/2200	205/2200
Torque, kg.m/rpm	63/1200	76/1400
Bore, mm	127	127
Stroke, mm	135	135
Swept volume, litres	10.26	10.26

Data on turbocharged truck engines, 1977

Type	DS8	DS11	DS14
Cylinders	6 inline	6 inline	8 in vee
Power, hp/rpm	210/2200	305/2100	375/2000
Torque, kg.m/rpm	70/1400	113/1300	151/1300
Bore, mm	115	127	127
Stroke, mm	125	145	140
Swept volume, litres	7.80	11.02	14.20

Data on the first Scania-Vabis direct-injection engines

Type	D420	D610-620	D810
Number of cylinders	4	6	8
Power at 2000 rpm, hp	90	135	180
Torque at 1200 rpm, kgm	34	51	68
Bore, mm	115	115	115
Stroke, mm	136	136	136
Swept volume, litres	5.65	8.47	11.30

In recent years new basic designs have not appeared as rapidly as they did in the past as economic conditions and tooling costs for high production prohibit such prolific design. But continuous development of existing designs goes on to meet ever increasing demands for higher power, lower noise, cleaner exhausts and better economy. For that purpose Scania established a large engine research laboratory overlooking the main Södertälje factory, complete with research test cells, noise chambers and masses of advanced data-analysis equipment. Adjacent to it is a test area with all kinds of road facilities for trucks and cross country vehicles. Special sections of the laboratory are devoted to transmission and structural design. In these labs Scania have developed their truck engines, the 8, 11 and 14 litre types, to a high degree of technical advancement, meeting all known world standards on emissions and noise, with very low fuel consumption, too.

Although Scania-Vabis traditionally turned out high quality commercial vehicles for domestic purposes in fairly large production batches, their engineering skill and inventiveness was always available to meet special requirements when they were called upon. Consequently, fire fighting vehicles, military vehicles, tanks, railcars, marine engines and a wide variety of industrial power units featured among the production from time to time.

The first fire fighting models were horse-drawn, but powerful pumps were driven by the type G42 engine which did such good service in the Vabis trucks. Impressive pumping demonstrations by these units led to a steady flow of orders from about 1906 onwards, especially in the growing Swedish townships where timber buildings presented a serious fire risk. It was not until just before the merger of Scania and Vabis in 1911 that complete, specially built motorised fire engines appeared, but once they did, some very spectacular types were made. One of the most advanced fire engines was a four-wheel-drive machine built in 1919 at the Malmö works, using the individual drive layout pioneered with the military trucks in 1916 (see Chapter 2). That machine was fast, stable and capable of reaching fires in the very worst road or winter conditions. After truck production was concentrated at Södertälje, fire engines continued to be built on modified truck or bus chassis, some with the company's own superstructures, others with imported turntables or escapes, including Metz and Magirus designs.

The Swedish armed forces were regular purchasers of both cars and trucks from the very earliest days, but the first special military vehicle was the four-wheel-drive machine built during the First World War to aid mobility in the poor conditions experienced in those northern latitudes for more than half the year. That was a successful venture both for Scania-Vabis and the army. A variety of vehicles based on the civilian designs but often with extra drive arrangements, including developments of the unique four-shaft drive layout, were provided right through the 1920s and 1930s. One of the most famous military vehicles built by Scania-Vabis was the SKP armoured truck, or 'Panzer Truck' as they were popularly known. During the Second World War 250 of these were built for the Swedish armed forces. So durable were they, and so well suited to the job, that 235 of them are still in use, many of them with the Swedish elements of the United Nations peace-keeping forces in various parts of the world. A small number of heavy armoured tanks were also made during the war, but few if any of those seem to have survived.

Cessation of hostilities in Europe did not mean the end of military vehicles however, and in 1956 a new cross country heavy truck, the 'Anteater', was built. Called LA82 in official parlance, these all-wheel-drive six wheelers were used as fighting vehicles, supply units, mobile command posts and many other military applications. A great number are still in use. In 1972 there was a further military demand for a heavy cross country truck capable of being driven in the worst conditions by conscript soldiers, and that meant automatic transmission. Scania developed suitable transmission and axle units with a unique type of automatic drive and the result was a truck of startling mobility. It was built in quantity in two and three-axle versions and is still in production. Civilian versions of these models were built too, mainly for exploration teams looking for oil and minerals, and for cross country cable maintenance work. That model, known as the SBAT, remains one of the finest cross country trucks in the world.

Industrial power units were always a profitable sideline ever since the merger in 1911 and a steady flow of engines for generators, pumping stations, marine installations and many other uses came from the Södertälje engine plant. But it was the D-series engines that really set Scania-Vabis up as a major supplier of industrial engines. Working in conjunction with Brown-Boveri in Switzerland, the eight-cylinder engine was developed as the first production turbocharged diesel in Europe — and possibly in the world — in which form it developed well over 200 horsepower, which was a lot of power in 1951. Such outputs seem puny by today's standards when automotive versions of the DS14 engine turn out 375 horsepower and industrial versions over 400 horsepower. But it is not only big power that is in demand. The little D8 engine in normal or turbocharged form is one of the most popular industrial engines, sold in thousands each year all over the world. In those sort of jobs they tend to go on working far longer than their counterparts in trucks, even though many of those manage a million kilometres.

Top Trucks were getting larger by the 1930s and one of the biggest four-wheelers at the turn of the decade was this seven tonne capacity 90 hp type.

Centre As late as 1928 some user preferred solid tyres, such was the state of roads in many areas. These three 3256 type trucks were delivered to a brewery in that year.

Bottom The appearance of the forward control bus chassis in 1931-32 led to a demand for a similar layout for trucks. Some were built on a slightly modified bus chassis with spacers between the frame and the body floor.

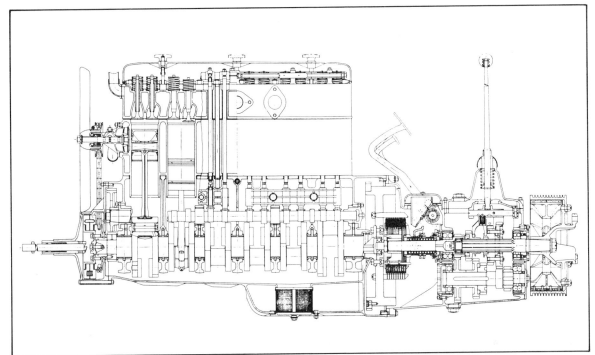

Above The last petrol engine before Hesselman and diesel types were adopted for heavy duty work was the 7.07 litre 110 hp type 1565, usually fitted with a four-speed gearbox and a big transmission brake.

Above left Sloping radiators added a touch of style from 1936. This type 3511 six-wheeler was rated at 17 tonnes, and had the 110 hp type 1565 engine, one of the last big petrol units.

Left The forward control bus chassis were particuarly suited for tipping work where compact dimensions were desirable. The first such chassis was designed and built in just three weeks and delivered to its buyer in August 1933.

Right In 1927 a new series of engines that were started on petrol and ran on crude oil were introduced. These were developed in conjunction with Jonas Hesselman. This was the type 1547 which remained in production until Scania's first true diesel engine appeared in 1936.

Left Production of the rationalised D-series direct injection diesels began in 1946, although design and development had begun in 1939. The range was available with four, six or eight cylinders and some were turbocharged. Long life was the engine's major attribute.

Below left The big type 16641 diesel engine went into production in 1936. It developed 120 hp and had indirect injection with heater plugs to aid starting.

Below The eight-cylinder 180 hp D-type was a big engine needing a long bonnet like the one on this 24 tonne quarry dumper of 1949.

Right One design detail of the D-series diesels involved taking cooling water out of the top of the cylinder heads instead of the side, as was customary. This contributed to the long service life. Another unique feature of the range was its ability to be assembled in 'right' or 'left-handed' versions.

Below right The type D815, launched in 1951, was the first batch-manufactured turbocharged diesel engine. The engine was rated at 205 hp and was designed for rail, bus, and marine application. Although similar in concept to the other D-series, this one is 'left-handed'.

The first experimental fire pump was hand-drawn, but with a four-cylinder Vabis petrol engine it pumped water well. Here it shows its paces at Stockholm harbour in 1906.

By 1907 horse drawn fire pumps were common, the sturdy Vabis four-cylinder G45 engine supplying the pumping power.

Inset Simplicity was the keynote of driving in the early days. But how many modern drivers could correctly identify all the items in the cab of this 1925 fire engine?

A Scania-Vabis fire chassis demonstrates its pumping power in Stockholm in 1914. Such performance was welcome in cities with a high proportion of wooden buildings.

A great step forward was represented by the motor fire engine. The town of Norrkoping took delivery of this 55 hp engine in 1912 which could travel to fires at the unprecendented speed of 50 kph.

From the mid-1920s, normal chassis were of sufficiently high performance for adaptation to fire fighters. This 1928 machine was built on a four ton truck chassis.

The 'limousine' type fire appliance made its appearance in Sweden as early as 1929. This one carried a 2000 litre water tank for quick action on arrival at a fire.

As late as 1938 there was distrust of big pneumatic tyres by fire authorities. This machine had semi-solid tyres to give stability to its 100 foot long Magirus escape. The chassis is basically a 33513 truck type.

Background photograph
The first four-wheel-drive military truck was built in
1916. Despite its cumbersome appearance it worked well
and the Swedish army bought several. In this picture the
prototype is under going trials, towing a normal truck
across country.

Inset
One of the first major military contracts was for 20 trucks
in 1916. In a ceremonial parade the vehicles were
delivered to the Crown Prince Hussars cavalry regiment.

DIESEL TRUCKS AND SPECIALIST VEHICLES

Left Armoured trucks built during the Second World War were called 'SKP-Panzer-trucks'. Of the 250 built during 1943-46, 235 are still in use, many with UN peace-keeping forces.

Right All-wheel-drive 20 tonne six wheelers developed in the early 1970s for the army formed a development platform for a heavy truck automatic transmission. With 270 hp and the automatic drive, performance of the SBAT was impressive. There was a two-axle version, too.

Below left Tanks were built in limited numbers during the Second World War, but they were never used in hostilities. This is a licence-built version of the Czecholovakian THNP light tank.

Below All-wheel-drive six wheelers built for the armed forces in 1956 were called 'Anteaters' because of their long noses; the official designation was LA82.

MEETING WORLD DEMANDS

After the cessation of world-wide hostilities in 1945 — in which Sweden was not directly involved although the supply situation meant restricted activity — it was clear that a major expansion of manufacturing capacity was required if Scania-Vabis was to stake a claim in the expanding world heavy vehicle markets that lay ahead. By the end of the war, thanks to substantial military contracts, the factory was capable of turning out about 1500 chassis a year. Several major expansion programmes took place, the first in 1948-49 when the direct injection diesels were launched which resulted in a production of around 4500 chassis by 1956, a little more than half of which were exported. South America was a major market and in 1953 local assembly began at Sao Paulo, Brazil. Scania subsequently established a full scale factory there in 1956, starting with engine manufacture while importing the other parts for local assembly, but that gave way gradually to 100 per cent local manufacture. A smaller plant operates at Tucuman in Argentina, serving that country and Uruguay.

Likewise in Europe, the EEC countries are served by two plants in Holland at Zwolle and nearby Meppel, which began production in 1963-64. Britain became another major market from the mid-1960s, but before that even, annual production was running at about 6500 chassis per annum. Australia provides a further big export market and many other countries are supplied from these major centres.

In the 1960s economic conditions dictated the merging of companies world-wide into bigger more diverse groups and Scania-Vabis was no exception. A merger was arranged with the Saab group which made passenger cars, aircraft, electronic gear including computers, and which also had control of the Nordarmatur heavy engineering company. The resulting group was called AB Saab-Scania and the name of Vabis was dropped after over 80 years of use in 1969. The headquarters of the Scania division of Saab-Scania, however, remained on the original site of the Vabis works of the 1890s and in fact there are still numerous artefacts around the older buildings to remind one of that bygone age. It is fitting in many ways that the Scania division still contributes a major share of the turnover and by far the largest proportion of the group's profits, and that that share has an upward trend as the 1970s draw to an end. The trend in truck power and weight is upwards too. In 1977 world-wide truck and bus production exceed 24,000 chassis with something like 10 per cent expansion expected before 1980.

Annual deliveries

	Trucks approx	Buses approx	Approx total no of vehicles
1910	40	0	150
1920	175	0	2,500
1930	130	110	4,500
1940	320	70	7,300
1950	1,320	440	16,100
1960	5,210	1,120	56,250
1970	9,610	915	152,200
1976	18,700	2,100	

Total world production in 1977 approx 24,000 vehicles.

The newest versions of heavy truck engines, the famous DS11 and DS14 types, develop their power at considerably lower engine speeds than their predecessors, giving substantially higher mid-speed torque. That means that with suitable gearing the trucks can maintain a good journey time without resorting to high road speeds, making up the difference by better acceleration and hill climbing. This concept has met with considerable success, especially in the 40 tonne range and above. These characteristics, coupled with extremely clean exhaust emissions and low noise, point the way to the expected trends in the years to come. There are developments in gas turbines and other power sources, but the efficiency of the advanced diesel engine is not expected to be superseded for many, many years according to Scania's engineers.

Further merger activity has been discussed, in particular with the Volvo group, but up to now no satisfactory terms have emerged as a basis for that action. However, the long term view appears to be that a united Swedish vehicle industry can only be a good thing when faced with the world manufacturing giants in the economic climate of the 1980s.

Below and top of page 64 In 1951 a Mack bus was imported by Scania-Vabis as part of a liaison agreement. It did extensive trials in Sweden—seen here in Stockholm mounting the pavement with a rear wheel. From it was developed the Scania-Vabis C-50 bus, forerunner of a long line of rear engined buses.

Right Top weight model in 1956 was the 6 x 4 180 hp LS71 tractive unit for 40 tonnes gross operation. Direct air brakes were fitted, and a ten-speed transmission incorporating a two-speed auxiliary box. Much of the engineering on this model was traded off with Mack in return for bus expertise.

Below left In 1954 new trucks with diesel engines and direct acting air brakes (those with their air reservoirs actually on the axles), began to emerge. First was the four wheel 12 ton L51 chassis with a new style front and treatment and the B420 direct injection engine.

Below and overleaf Concurrently with the introduction of the 10.25 litre D10 diesel in 1958, a new range of trucks with that engine and unit-construction cab and front end was launched. These were the famous 75-series trucks which became an immediate success.

Opposite and top of page 68 After the D11 and DS11 engines were developed from the D10, a new and powerful range of trucks was introduced known as the 76 series. They had turbocharged 220 hp engines, ten-speed gearboxes and were offered either as the L76 with a normal cab or LB76 with forward control. Many of these models, built from 1963 onwards, are still working all over the world.

Right A new highly automated assembly factory at Södertälje was started in the mid-1960s and now turns out over 18000 chassis a year.

Below One of the smallest modern Scanias was the L50, which used the D7 engine. A later version, the L55 used the D8 diesel. Gross weight was 10 tonnes.

Opposite A significant development in bus design was the 'hush-bus', a very quiet version of the CR111 introduced in 1971. The engine was fully enclosed and lined with sound-absorbing panels. It also had a very acute turning circle, and could clear another vehicle parked one metre in front.

Right Scania-Vabis did a lot of groundwork before opening up new markets. Here a group of British hauliers tour the Swedish factory in 1965, well before Scanias were available in Britain. They include Mr Ken Beresford of Stoke on Trent, John Smillie the Glasgow haulier, Fred Robinson of Stockton-on-Tees, David McVeigh and Bill Alston.

Below Italian market models are fitted with cast spoked wheels instead of the common European type of pressed steel wheels.

Left Most popular models in Brazil are the relatively simple four wheelers. This is a locally built L76.

Right When the 110 series trucks were introduced in 1968 they represented new high standards in trucking, not only with their high performance engines, but in safety and comfort, too.

Below left Australia is a bus market for Scania. Chassis are shipped out to be fitted with local coachwork, like this example by Athol Hedges of Brisbane.

Below Cab interiors on the 110 series Scanias in 1968 were very comfortable for that period. This is a very early example which still had a separate lever for the splitter part of the gearbox. Later models had an air-switch on the main lever.

Left The DS11 engine, heart of all the 110, and 111 series buses and trucks, was a conventional design made outstanding by careful attention to engineering and combustion system detail.

Right Swedish safety regulations specified brutal strength tests which made Scanias famous and desirable the world over. Here a one tonne weight slams into a screen pillar.

Below Elaborate production facilities include test cells where every engine, like this DS14, is put through live power tests and bedded in before delivery.

Above In Britain, the LB110 Scania probably did more to advance truck driving and operating standards than any other type after it was introduced in 1968.

Opposite Scania's 14 litre V8 engine, introduced in 1969, used new techniques both in turbocharging and combustion as well as new methods in its production. Latest versions of it turn out 375 hp with extremely high torque at low speeds.

Right Feature of the modern Scania cab is that the main step is enclosed by the door, keeping it free of ice and snow.

Background photograph Scanias tend to handle well in the snow, as the author discovered on a visit to Sweden some years ago.

Top inset Air deflectors are frequently fitted to the cab corners to help prevent road spray from obscuring the mirrors and side windows.

Bottom inset Normal Scania practice on current forward control cabs is to provide access to auxiliaries through the front grille panel. Note the roller blind at the base of the radiator, which aids quick warm-up.

Left and right The normal control 140 was perhaps the most purposeful looking truck built in recent years. It had the 350 hp V8 engine, boosted to 375 hp in the 141-145 model introduced in 1977. The cab is an 80/81 model shell with a glassfibre bonnet.

Below left Scanias are a common sight on the international meat trade routes from Ireland. This big 140 is normally driven by Isobel Millar, 4ft 9in tall daughter of the fleet owner.

Below The ten-speed synchro-mesh gearbox, fitted as standard in Scanias of the 1970s, tends to be somewhat buried beneath chassis hardware.

Left Australia has been a good market for Scanias with specially developed models. To meet the local regulations the front axle was mounted further forwards than usual.

Right The 275 bhp LB111 series operates equally well as an articulated tractor (see back cover) or with a drawbar trailer and proved equally popular with hauliers and own-account users.

Below right Working 24 hours a day this British 1970 Scania LB80 covered a million miles — 1.6 million kilometres — in seven years in the fleet of Arthur Turnbull of Erdington, Birmingham.

Below Six-wheeled version of the LB81 was labelled LB86 and made an extremely fast, stable and rigid truck ideally suited, like this one on the Scotland-London route, to shipping fresh meat over many hundreds of kilometres.

Good social conditions and working
environments are a feature both
inside and outside the Scania
factory at Södertälje.

Left The economy and performance of the LB81, introduced in 1975, earned it a good place in many markets including Britain.

Overleaf The DS8 engine is compact but develops a healthy 205 horsepower, enough to propel a 32 ton truck over all classes of road.

Below left One of the first Scania-Vabis LB76 trucks in Britain began work in the spring of 1967 and is still in daily use with its original owner, Jubilee Transport. There were 15 Scanias in the fleet by 1977.

Below Not a short wheelbase chassis but a convenient way of shipping front and rear sub sections for incorporating into integral bodywork in export markets.

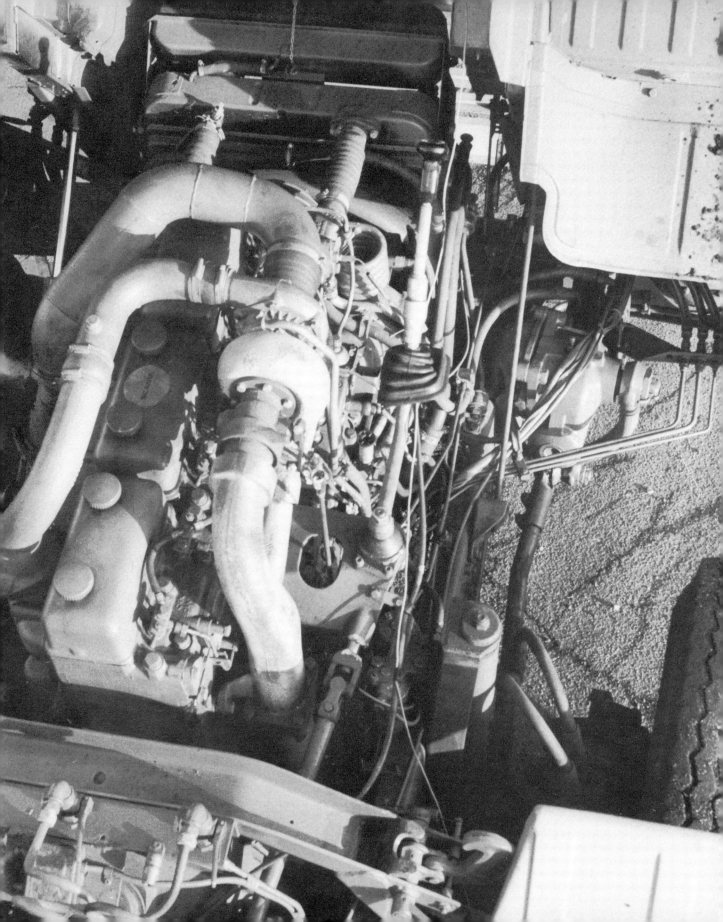